Hoodwinked I

Constitutional Issues

"As things stand, the U.S. Constitution was never amended to sub-classify property, permitting open-ended taxation of private homes and cars by municipalities."

* * *

"Personally, I understand free K-to-12, but rather than local property taxes, states need to pay for K-to-12 with income and sales taxes originated by their legislatures – the way all social programs are paid for."

ISBN: 978-1-7330672-1-8   [Paperback Edition]

Please visit *hoodwinked.net* for video versions of this manuscript.
Printed and bound in The United States of America.

Published by LittleHouse Enterprises Inc.

LittleHouse
ENTERPRISES

Hoodwinked

The Illegal Taxation of Private American Homes

Vol. I - Constitutional Issues

J.A. PATRINA

Hoodwinked

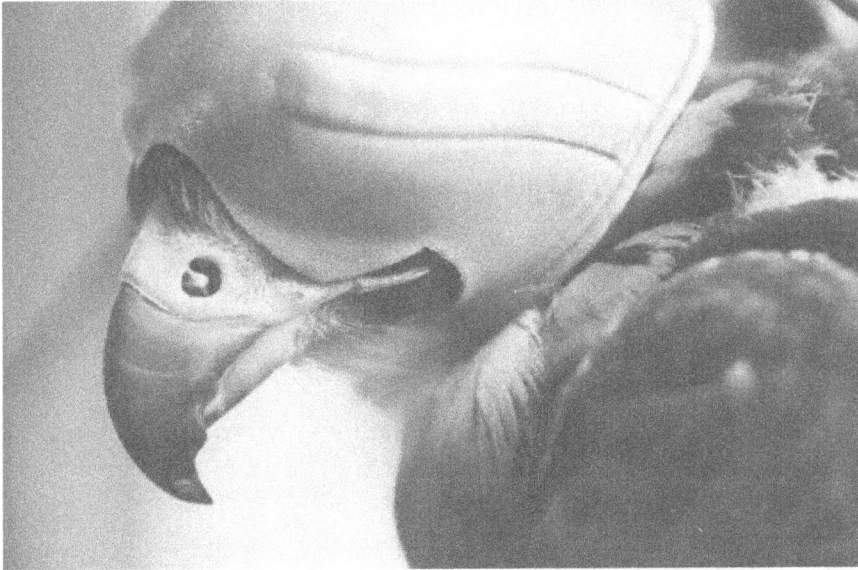

To be hoodwinked is to be deceived. The term actually derives from the practice of placing a hood over the head of a **falcon** in the Middle Ages when engaged in the **sport** of falconry. This practice **tricked** the falcon into believing it was nighttime, thus calming the bird so that one could recover the **prey** from the bird's talons - **Urban Dictionary**

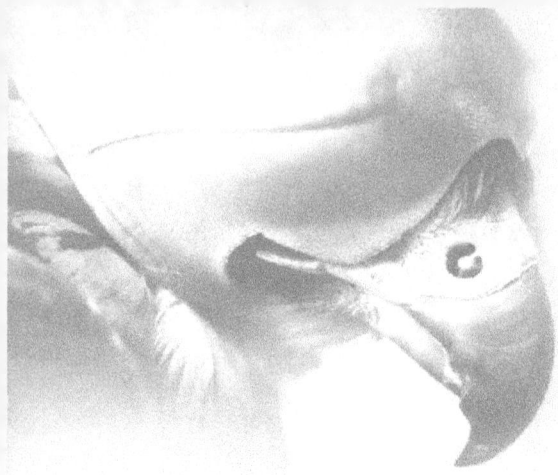

THE BASIC CONSTITUTIONAL ISSUES
How We Were Hoodwinked

Who has Authority to Originate Taxes?

- Legislatures Only – As Per the Constitution's *Origination Clause*
- This Authority Cannot Be Delegated - Town Voting to Levy Tax is Unlawful

What Tax Types are Lawful?

- *Direct* on Property, If Equally Apportioned for Homes & Cars, and
- *Indirect* on Commercial Activity – A Percent of Sales, Income, Profits & Tolls
- *Assessment-Based* Home Taxation is Neither Direct or Indirect – It is Unlawful
- *Dormant Homes* Do Not Generate Taxable Income – Nothing to Tax

What Do State Tax Codes Apply To?

- Only to *Lawful* Direct & Indirect Taxes, and
- Not to Unlawful Assessment Based Property and Wealth Taxes

- Tax Collection Procedures Must Follow Due Process, with *Judicial Oversite*
- *Non-Judicial* Tax Sale "Taking" to Collect Tax is Unlawful

What Are the Home Owner's Overall Rights?

- Inalienable Natural Rights to Property.
- Rights Granted by the U.S. Constitution Cannot Be Taken Away
- Citizens Enjoy Absolute Rights to Property, Except in Cases Of …
- Crime, Eminent Domain, Intestate (No Heirs) & Equal Direct Taxes
- Legislatures Cannot Pass New Laws to Extend These Exceptions

Who Should Pay for Free K-to-12 Education?

- The State Legislative Body Who Mandated It
- Funded via Constitutional State Income & Sales Taxes
- A Practice Already Done Today with Low-Income School Districts

Who Should Pay to Operate State Administrative Laws (Code)?

- The Legislative Body Who Mandated These
- By Paying for Local Building, Zoning, EPA & Fire Employees
- Funded via State Income & Sales Taxes, Funds Pro-rated Down

Who Should Pay for Local Police & Roads?

- The Local Households Who Use These
- Funded via *Equally Apportioned* Direct Property Taxes
- Less Than $1,000 per Household in Connecticut

The Hoodwinked Books

There are three (3) "Hoodwinked" books authored by Joe Patrina, the first constitutionally oriented, the second historically oriented, and the third personally (anecdotally) oriented.

Within these separate orientations, the books explore the natural, constitutional rights to private property held by all American citizens. This book, *Volume I Constitutional Issues,* deconstructs the unlawful home taxation tactics state governments use to fund social programs such as *free K-to-12 education*, but as a remedy, it suggests how to fund state mandates within U.S. Constitutional constructs.

- *Hoodwinked Volume I – Constitutional Issues*
- *Hoodwinked Volume II – Historical Perspective*
  The Arc of Land Ownership Rights from Old England
  to 1620 Plymouth, to the American Revolution, to Modern Times
- *Hoodwinked Volume III – Code – The Debasing of America*

The Author, **Joe Patrina,** is a singer/songwriter based in Connecticut. As with his songwriting, Joe applies his seasoned observational skills and to-the-point writing style to pen insightful works on sports, history, politics, medicine, music, and law.

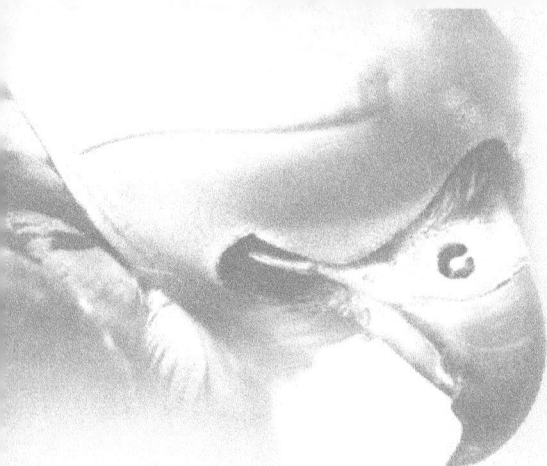

PRIMER

A SUPREME COURT INTERVENTION STRATEGY PROTECTING PROPERTY

The Origination, Taking, Equal Protection,
Due Process & Direct Taxation Clauses of the U.S. Constitution.

By J.A. Patrina

At heart, American private property is supposed to be sacrosanct. "What's mine is actually mine – not up for grabs".

To affirm property, the Constitution authorizes legislatures alone to levy taxes but only so long as they are tied to transactional events such as sales, income, capital gains and tolls ... not to property. After paying these, what's left is yours, your home, your castle.

But is it yours, when under the threat of confiscation, municipalities extort monies from you each year? Certainly, this is not owning property "free and clear" as the Founders intended. We were Hoodwinked.

Currently, socialist voices are looking to go beyond home taxation, advocating taxation on any kind of property – even financial wealth. This metastasis needs to be arrested by The U.S. Supreme Court (SCOTUS), full stop. *Hoodwinked I* presents the Constitutional framework for achieving a vivid demarcation line. Below, the topic's "primer".

Let's deconstruct what happened.

Municipalities are just regular corporations. Like the McDonalds Hamburger Corporation, they were never granted taxation or taking authority.

Instead, the U.S. Constitution's "Origination Clause" specifies that taxes-in-any-form need to originate in the legislature – taxing authority cannot be delegated to local budget voting.

The property tax phenomenon, which evolved in earnest after the Civil War, blossoming in recent decades through billowing government school budgets, has never been challenged. As things stand, the U.S. Constitution was never amended to classify private homes taxable, permitting open-ended extortion by municipalities.

Such an amendment would repudiate the whole "We the People" foundation, placing us and our property subordinate to the government.

Instead, to circumvent this conundrum, and without a court battle being waged over legal standing, State Legislatures invented tax lien/confiscation extortion devices which simply ignore Constitutional protections of private property, and force unilateral obligations onto citizens to pay any amount demanded.

What money is actually owed?

Other than local road usage and police, residents do not implicitly *contract* for town corporate services, nor do homeowners owe "residency" rents for property they already own, nor do homeowners earn "taxable income" on their *dormant homes*. So, what gives?

State legislatures pass unconstitutional law, judges rule unconstitutionally, and local mayors operate unchecked. Unless challenged at the U.S. Constitutional level, these illegal practices are emboldened, crushing the natural, sacred rights of the citizens. Ultimately, people's homes are taken without court oversight.

The founders set up a system to prevent all of this corruption, but somehow, the worst violators of the U.S. Constitution became the States, who now seem a wall separating common citizens from their U.S. Constitutional protections.

Life, liberty and Property Are Natural Rights

State home taxation habits and local tax collectors, therefore, must be confronted at the U.S. Constitution level, as home taxation wantonly tramples our *natural rights* to life, liberty and property – the bedrock of American law.

And recall, our rights to life, liberty and property sit *inalienable*— neither able to be given away nor taken from us by any operation of government, including by enacting new statutory laws.

In defiance of these absolute rights, home taxation side-steps *legislative authority*, ignores *contract law*, and abandons *due process* altogether, the firewall protecting against government overreach. Home taxation represents a subjugation of *originalist* American liberty by *socialist* interests.

So, to be Constitutional, social mandates—like free K-to-12 education—must be funded via legislatively-approved, state-wide, transactional-based taxes, with pooled monies pro-rated down to *all* towns, reflecting *equal protection* across all student head counts.

In detail, the author's Hoodwinked I, II & III book series examines property rights from biblical times to today and calls upon U.S. Constitutional law to reverse home *taxation*, pushing *mandate, funding and equal protection responsibilities* back up to the state legislatures where they belong.

Again, Constitutional compliance remains paramount. And though you may say pushback on home taxation amounts to tilting at windmills, I invite you to more deeply explore these pivotal Constitutional issues, at *Hoodwinked.net.*

Next, the question becomes: What is to be done?

First, realize that based upon the language of the relevant U.S. Constitutional clauses, municipal taxation operates unlawfully at every turn. Neither *assessment-based* property taxes - propped up by town voting - nor *non-judicial tax collection "taking"* practices stand under the U.S. Constitution. These practices cannot be "tweaked"; they need to end.

Who, then, you might ask, should pay for free K-to-12, Police & Roads?

In Connecticut, for example, free K-to-12 education is settled law, incorporated within the Connecticut constitution back in 1965. Free K-to-12 is fine, but how it is currently paid for is unlawful.

Rather than homes, funding needs to occur through state-level sales and income taxes - *originated* within the state legislature and pro-rated down to the municipalities in *equally protected* allotments per student, used not just for government schools but at one's school of choice.

And who, then, should pay for local roads and police?

The local households who use these, funded via *equally apportioned direct* property/pol taxes, less than $900 per household in Connecticut, or around $150 per person. Everything gets covered, but funded Constitutionally, preserving property as "free and clear", with the annual $150 a minor service charge, very much like a utility bill.

A Test Case

I decided not to pay property taxes in 2018, to experience the reaction of my town, *the Town of Simsbury.* I found the manner the town coerces the tax – *non-judicial tax sales* – to certainly violate *due process* at its core, as it by-passes the courts all together, while also ignoring the 5th amendment's narrow *taking* clause, which promises *just compensation* for eminent domain takes, with no other taking sanctioned.

Without judicial review, *tax sales* simply put your house up for a quick sale to cover back taxes, the owner left with little or nothing. Raw taking, happening in many states!

Whose Town Is It?

My goal is to enlist town officials to correct their unlawful practices, to have them defend us, the homeowners – it's their job!

At heart, I am looking for legal protection by my town against the State of Connecticut's unlawful home and automobile taxation practices, the same way the town's police force protects me from physical crime. After all, town corporations were created to serve the interests and protect the rights of local residents; not to be enforcers of unconstitutional state constructs.

In behalf of its citizens, the Town is obligated to take the Connecticut Governor to Federal Court … to force the State into funding both its K-to-12 *and* administrative code mandates without extorting households, and to pro-rate State-collected monies down to each town in an "equal protection" manner.

Upon judgement for the plaintiff citizens, the State of Connecticut would be ordered to rebalance its revenue sources, forgoing home taxation and instead boosting *legislatively approved* sales and income taxes, taxes that stand up to real representative, voter scrutiny. This precedent would then carry to the other states.

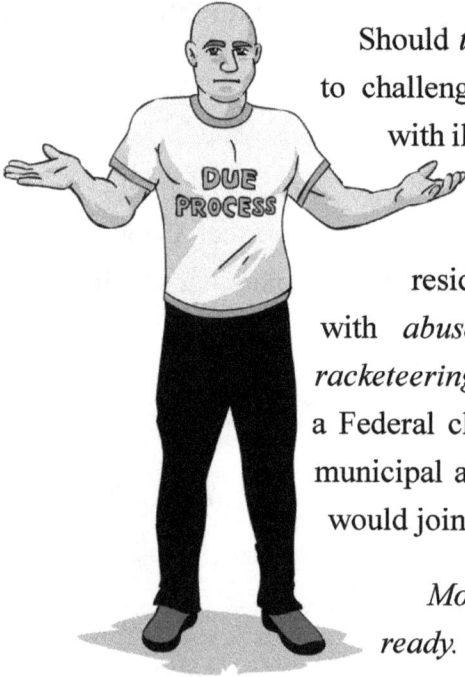

Should *the Town of Simsbury* decide not to challenge the state and instead persist with illegal tax practices, local officials perpetrating Constitutional fraud against their own residents may be criminally charged with *abuse of power* and institutional *racketeering*. Citizens would need to start a Federal class action suit against both the municipal and state co-conspirators. Many would join.

More importantly, SCOTUS is ready.

The "Knick versus the Township of Scott, Pennsylvania" Case

A 2019 decision by the U.S. Supreme Court invites bringing property cases directly to Federal Court.

Until 2019, property owners had to go through State Courts, (that generally protect the State). In summarizing the Rose Mary Knick case, Chief Justice Roberts wrote:

"We now conclude that the state litigation requirement imposes an unjustifiable burden on a property owner's claim that his or her land has been effectively taken for public benefit without the government paying just compensation."

Property owners are entitled to adjudication in Federal Court if they can prove constitutional rights have been violated.

Our Law of the Land

The U.S. Constitution's intent to protect *absolute rights for property* stands a centerpiece to America's founding, and neither popular voting nor government legislation can authorize wealth taking from one's home, bank account, investment portfolio, or any other asset. To go after property, socialist need to retire the United States itself, and post a new constitution.

And yes, as in the Old South, modern municipalities have built entire economic systems around the home enslavement practice. Though one can advocate for liberal social programs, if to pay for these you directly interfere in the lives and properties of citizens, then you cross the line into de facto socialism—a form of enslavement.

But an engrained, now metastasizing home taxation cancer habit does not make it acceptable. As with full slavery, it is again time to stand for natural rights.

The Supreme Court needs to strike down taxation of private property and put American liberty back on the map.

A Supreme Court stance repudiating home taxation effectively creates a bulwark similar to the 1800's anti-slavery amendments, this time blocking property confiscation in America …"home subjugation" ended, with "individual liberty" preserved.

A line would be drawn. *In the American system, personal homes and financial properties are both off limits to government encumbrance.* Life, liberty and property would be re-affirmed as inalienable natural rights unable to be subjugated by *any* operation of government.

"Free and clear" property, the ultimate battle ground. Your input protecting American liberty through this strategy will be appreciated. Please reach out.

Details:
Hoodwinked.net.

Contents

Part I

The Constitutional Framework Surrounding Property Tax

One's right to life, liberty and property are considered natural rights in the American system, sitting beyond the reach of government. So long as one does not engage in criminal behavior, one's natural rights are inalienable, meaning they cannot be given or taken away.

Limits to One's Rights to Property

As things stand today, constitutionally, absent of crime or contractual arrangements between individuals and government bodies, one's rights to property still sit above the reach of government, except in four (4) spelled-out instances, to wit:

Crime	Government can obtain search-and-seizure warrants from judges if there is *compelling* evidence that crime or injury

to others is taking place on someone's private property.

Eminent Domain	Under eminent domain, property can be taken, but only for real public use, e.g., to build a highway, so long as the owner is paid fair value (not quick sales tax auction value).
Intestate	Government can absorb (inherit) property upon the death of a property owner who does not have a will and with no beneficiaries, and
Direct Tax Apportionment	Should government ever directly tax individuals or their property, the tax is first to be approved by the legislature and the tax charge apportioned equally amongst the people (not variable taxes based upon assessed values).

Even these four (4) aforementioned powers granted to government can only be pursued through *due process*, and not via *unilateral* decree. So with this said, is there room in the constitution to tax private property at all? The answer: yes, but narrowly.

Two Types of Taxation Are Permitted – Indirect & Direct

The U.S. Constitution grants Congress authority to levy taxes in just two ways, with states also constrained accordingly.

Indirect Taxes – On commercial activity (sales, income, profits, tolls), called "indirect" — as the individual has some control over one's activity, e.g., one can choose not to buy, one can choose to take back roads.

During the dormant years of ownership, one's home and vehicle properties are not commercially active, making no money, and hence they don't fall under government indirect taxation authority. When the property is sold, becoming commercially active, the transaction might trigger an indirect conveyance tax.

Direct Taxes - On people for being alive (poll taxes), and on property for being owned (real estate and personal property, such as homes and cars). These "unseemly" direct cases leave the individual no discretion. It's "Pay or Else!"

Should a legislature ever wish to levy a direct tax on life itself or on dormant, paid-for property, it can do so, but only within the constraints of the U.S. Constitution's two (yes, *two*) **Direct Taxation Apportionment** clauses:

Article 1, Section 2, Clause 3 cites: *the federal government is prohibited from imposing direct (property or poll) taxes* unless such *taxes* are then given to the states in proportion to population.

Article 1, Section 9, Clause 4 states: *No Capitation, or other direct Tax shall be laid, unless in Proportion to the Census (or enumeration herein) before directed to be taken.* Through the authority of the Fourteenth Amendment, these two clauses apply to all levels of government.

Furthermore, equal tax apportionment is backed up by the U.S. Constitution's 14th Amendment **Equal Protection** clause demanding equal treatment of citizens under the law (no tax deals).

The Rules for Legal Taxation

Generally speaking, the *state legislature* has the power to assess, levy and collect taxes for general or special purposes on all property, subjects or objects which may be *lawfully* taxed. *Note the qualifiers "legislature" and "lawfully"— here explained.*

> The U.S. Constitution's **Origination Clause** cites that *"All Bills for raising Revenue shall originate in the House of Representatives."* Only federal and state legislatures can levy taxes. Taxation authority cannot be delegated by states to town voting or to individual "czars", where citizen votes, or executive decree — rather than legislative votes - are used to levy taxes of any kind.

> The **Substantive Due Process** clause of the 14th Amendment *prohibits the federal and state governments, respectively, from depriving any person of life, liberty, or property, without due process* of law. The states are constrained by *all* federal limitations, including due process.

Non-Judicial-Takes Defy Due Process

Besides Simsbury's assessment-based taxation having no legal foundation whatsoever, Simsbury's "tax sale confiscation" of private homes to collect said unlawful tax bypasses judicial due process, making these *non-judicial-takes* a clear violation of both aspects of U.S. Constitutional *due process:*

> **procedural due process** which places limitations on the manner in which a law is administered, applied, or enforced,

> **substantive due process** which prohibits the government from infringing on fundamental constitutional liberties.

Connecticut's Own Constitutional Protections

Locally, even the **Connecticut Constitution** speaks to these same principles: *All men when they form a social compact, are equal in rights; and no man or set of men are entitled to exclusive public emoluments or privileges from the community ...* These statements can be applied to forbid unequal tax and government service treatments throughout the state and within each municipality.

Municipalities Force Contracts on Citizens

Procedurally, **The Obligation of Contract** clause (Article 1, Section 10, Clause 1) prohibits states from interfering in any contracts its citizens engage in. Yet with home and vehicle property taxes, the state specifically interferes *by imposing a contract* upon the citizen, turning the citizen into a reluctant "consumer" of unspecified goods and services, and forcing a recurring debt obligation upon that consumer.

States Must Comport to U.S. Constitutional Law

Ultimately, **the 14ᵗʰ Amendment of the U.S. Constitution** proclaims that any limitation placed against the Federal government also applies downstream to states and municipalities. All of the above-mentioned limitations need to be factored into how states pay for state-mandated programs, such as "free K-to-12 education".

As well, the **Privileges and Immunities Clause** of Article IV, Section 2 of the Constitution states that "the citizens of each state shall be entitled to all privileges and immunities of citizens in the several states." This clause refers to one's fundamental rights, such as due process and one's natural rights to life, liberty and property. No operation of state government can dismantle these inalienable rights.

Conclusion

The Town of Simsbury uses neither indirect nor direct taxation approaches, and without constitutional standing, has concocted a third way of taxing based upon the perceived value of property. The town levies this assessed-value tax without legislative voting and without following the rules of due process.

Because states and towns cannot create authority outside the bands of the U.S. Constitution, and cannot ignore the due process protections afforded citizens, Simsbury's home taxation practice is unconstitutional at every turn – no matter how many state statutes are written to wiggle around this.

Footnote: In 1913, the Income Tax Amendment was engineered to specifically give government the right to use *non-apportioned formulas* in concocting *income tax* schemes. No such exception to apportionment was ever made for *property*. More, no direct property taxes have been ruled upon or sanctioned by the U.S. Supreme Court since the passing of the *substantive due process* clause of the 14th Amendment in 1868.

With the above said, we can next consider the question: who is to pay for the roads we drive on? This question is answered in *Part II – The Legal Remedy for Funding Local Roads, Police and State Programs Like Public Education.*

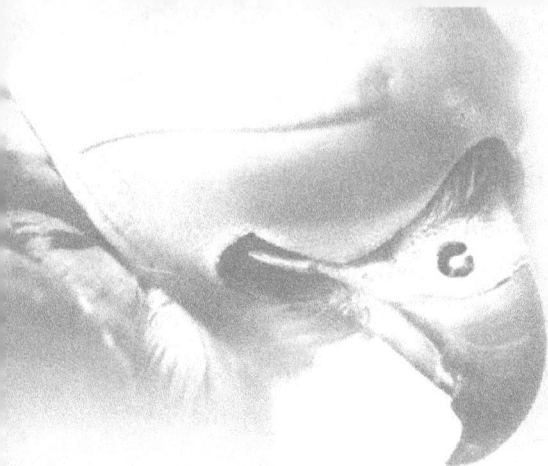

Part II

The Legal Remedy for Funding Local Roads, Police, and State Programs Like Public Education.

As mentioned, the state legislature can directly tax private property if the tax is apportioned equally. Below, the town's core roads/police overhead (a big worry of many) is appropriately paid for via a direct home taxation sum of $866 per household, a very low burden. Analysis:

- There are 9,000 homes and apartments in Simsbury
- $3.7 million current budget for roads - $411 per household
- $4.1 million current budget for police - $455 per household...

This totals a $7.8 million "direct taxation" budget – of just $866 per household.

Education, Fire, Building and Zoning— all state mandated programs— need to be underwritten by the state legislature which approved the programs, funded via *legislatively approved* sales and income taxes, as per the U.S. Constitution's *Origination Clause*, and pro-rated back down to the towns, the way the state currently funds low-income school districts today. This Constitutionally sound scenario, as designed by the founders, will also restore a political dynamic that moderates government spending.

HOODWINKED seeks to push mandate, funding and equal protection responsibilities back up to the state legislature where they legally belong.

As background, by accepting home taxation in the late 1800's, towns became *duped* into operating illegal taxation schemes so that the state's legislative body stayed *politically shielded* from the mandates for which its representatives voted.

This was achieved by corrupting Connecticut's Title 12 Tax Code, as described in *Part III – Today's Unlawful Application of Title 12 – The Tax Code*.

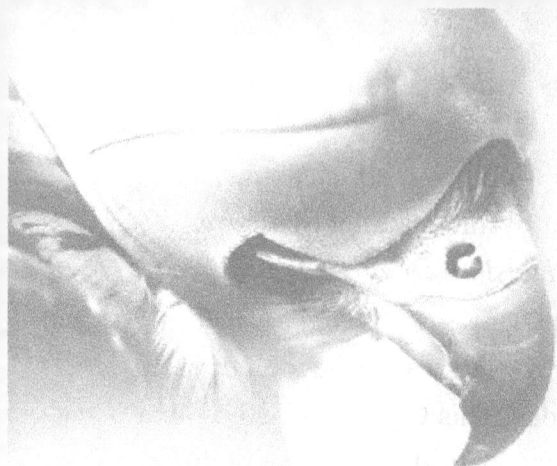

Part III

Today's Unlawful Application of CT Title 12 –
The Tax Code

Before discussing "Title 12 - TAXES", one first considers *Connecticut General Statute (CGS) 47-1 regarding property rights,* passed way back in 1793, still in force.

This key statute recognizes that home owners possess *absolute* rights to property, and that a*bsolute* property rights can only be made *conditional* based upon a direct apportioned tax being sanctioned by the legislature.

The CGS Title 12 taxation series passed in 1875 lays out the procedural rules for *lawful* tax collection. Title 12 neither retired "absolute" rights to property, nor did it grant U.S. Constitutional authority for the towns to tax private property using the *assessed value* method. Title 12 solely pertains to the collection of lawful taxes whether indirect commercial or direct apportioned in nature – *but the collected taxes must be lawful in the first place!*

Absent of any direct tax program in Connecticut today, the Title 12 tax collection series effectively only applies to authorized indirect taxes, such as sales, income, fees, tolls, etc. Real property and homes fall outside of its jurisdiction as assessed-value taxation is unlawful, and dormant property earns no income.

By claiming Title 12 applicable to unlawful, assessment-value based taxes, town authorities manufacture false authority, and this coloring confuses citizens, making abusive debt collection practices (such as non-judicial taking of homes) appear legitimate, tricking citizens into paying unlawful taxes.

It is this misuse of Title 12 that leads to necessary federal statutory provisions designed to blunt such abuse, described next in *Part IV – Federal Statutory Law That May Relate to the Behavior of Municipalities.*

Part IV

Federal Statutory Law That May Relate to the Behavior of Municipalities

The Fair Debt Collection Practices Act (FDCPA) was designed by the Congress in 1977 to protect consumers from abusive debt collection practices.

FDCPA includes provisions where *debt needs to be proven* (a bill of sale, etc.), where rules and rights cannot be confusing for "the least sophisticated consumer" and where the mistreated individual is entitled to real damages, statutory damages, *and attorney's fees.*

With town invoices, the tax collector alleges that property owners hold accounts with the town (which they do not), owing home and vehicle debts, treating them as consumers, yet providing neither…

    a) commercial agreement papers entered between citizens and the municipality, nor

b) bill of sale papers proving a debt was actually triggered via a transactional exchange, as the law demands.

Instead, the town *unilaterally* imposes invented consumer accounts and debt obligations on its citizens, with the threat of using town corporate powers to tow vehicles and to auction homes unless *unproven* debt demands are met. This extortion device confuses "the least sophisticated consumer" into paying monies for an invented debt.

Color-of-Law - Under color-of-law, state and town workers cannot create the appearance of authority in order to intimidate home owners into anything, including paying unlawful property taxes.

Section 242 of Title 18 makes it a crime for a person, e.g., a town employee, acting under color of any law to willfully deprive a person of a right or privilege protected by the Constitution or laws of the United States. Punishments consist of fines and imprisonment.

The Federal Racketeering Act – Under the "Racketeer Influenced and Corrupt Organizations Act" (RICO), government agents cannot operate institutional muscle to coerce citizens into anything, including into paying unlawful property taxes.

RICO was created in 1970 to protect citizens from the tactic of using an enterprise (such as The Town of Simsbury, Inc.) to conduct illegal activity.

To be guilty of racketeering, an insider must violate two of the following crimes: *mail fraud, wire fraud, obstruction of state or federal law enforcement, extortion, monetary transactions in property derived from unlawful activities, or sale of stolen property.*

The punishment for violating the criminal provisions of RICO are fines and sentences of up to 20 years for each offense.

Town officials need to be mindful of these statutes, as regardless of the validity of assessment-based, budget-voting-approved property taxation, these operating behaviors could be deemed unlawful by the Department of Justice.

Next, we look at what transpired as a result of the author *not* paying property taxes in 2017 and 2018 (until forced to under duress of losing my property), described in *Part V – The Peculiar Interaction Between Myself and the Local Tax Collector Regarding Plans to Use a Non-Judicial Tax Sale to Liquidate My Property.*

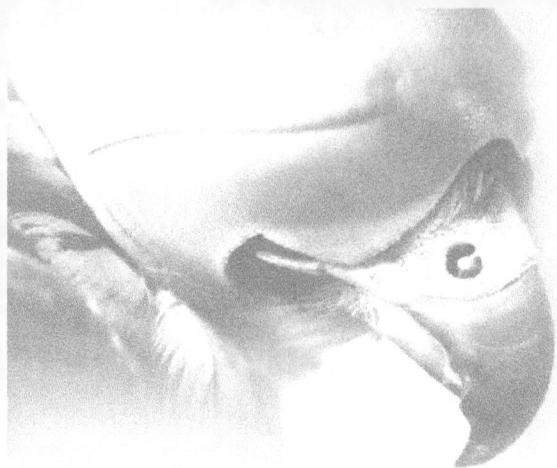

Part V

The Peculiar Interaction Between Myself and the Local Tax Collector Regarding Plans to Use a "Non-Judicial Tax Sale" to Liquidate My Property

In 2018, I met twice with the Tax Collector of the Town of Simsbury, once in the early summer to exchange ideas and subsequently in September after she mailed a "tax sale" notice, causing me to meet her regarding the possible loss of my house.

In the first meeting, initially, we exchanged pleasantries about my 91-year-old mother, as we had common friends ever since childhood and she knew my mom well.

But the thrust of the first meeting dealt with me explaining why I had not paid the tax. I described the various constitutional constructs and she appeared to understand them. In particular, she grasped the concept that while owned, homes sit dormant earning no money upon which to levy a tax. But as I added "that once active – and a home is sold" - she jumped in saying that "a sales conveyance tax could be applied at that point". At this moment I had a bit of hope that she accepted the whole concept, but no.

In that first meeting, the Tax Collector soon added that she was considering a "Tax Sale" approach rather than "a foreclosure process involving Judges", as a Tax Sale would be a more efficient way to collect taxes for the Town. At the time, I did not register what she described, as I always assumed a judge is involved in any dispute over property. I guess we had a nice, if unproductive meeting, and said our good-byes.

This led to the second meeting, which came about as soon as the Tax Collector mailed me a notice threatening me and my wife with a "Tax Sale" of the said property we had worked our whole lives for.

I made an appointment to see her, and brought my friend, attorney Arnold Sholovitz, to help navigate the situation, a trusted lawyer by many in Simsbury, personally known by the Tax Collector. We wanted to discover what had transpired to embolden her to implement such a home liquidation threat upon a longstanding citizen.

The second meeting started cordial, though it caused my coffee cup hand to tremble in what I soon heard. As reported by the Tax Collector, at some point after our first meeting, she managed to get official consent from the town manager, the finance manager, and all six of the town's selectmen to go ahead with the aforementioned "Tax Sale" procedure, *which notably skips the inconvenient step of judges weighing in on foreclosure arguments.*

Instead, the municipality puts an ad in the paper and "quick sells" the house, brazenly keeping monies they claim, leaving the homeowner abandoned to fight off the buyer over title – as the Town had no title to sell in the first place.

Upon request, the Tax Collector handed Attorney Sholovitz the Town endorsement memorandums encouraging her to proceed. This is when my hand started shaking, not due to fear, but more, due to the complete dismissal by every local bureaucrat, many who I knew, of the sanctity of Due Process of Law, a pillar of America, a pillar of England since the Magna Carta.

The Tax Collector, my mother's friend, just did not get it, and this was no time to elucidate upon the property right principles of the founders. I soon left, temporarily heart-broken that a fellow American with government power could miss the big picture, and worse, that all of her colleagues in local government had missed the big picture as well.

They had all, willingly, entered a dark place that none would want had they the prior chance to read this document. They led each other astray. What to do? As the James Taylor song goes "It used to be my town, too".

Ok, though constitutional abandonment by local political leaders is heartbreaking, lets dig into a few Supreme Court rulings on *property taking*. Recall, there are no *property tax* cases with the Supreme Court because, as explained, until the summer of 2019, property issues were adjudicated by State courts.

The Judge Roberts invitation written for the 2019 *Rose Mary Knick* case, hopefully opens the door for the top court to someday soon deliberate upon the constitutional underpinnings of *property tax* itself.

Part VI

Supreme Court Case Law Related to
Due Process in the Taking of Property

The following is a sampling of Supreme Court rulings regarding the unwarranted taking of property and the failure to follow due process.

Connecticut v. Doehr (1991)

The attachment of real property has a significant adverse effect on the owner's rights over the property. It inhibits selling or transferring title, undermines the owner's credit rating, clouds title, complicates the prospect of obtaining a loan or mortgage, and can result in a default on an existing mortgage. Since it was attached before the case was heard, there was a substantial risk of error. The plaintiff did not have a significant interest that would support infringing on the defendant's right to have a hearing on whether the attachment was appropriate, especially since there was no suggestion that the defendant was about to transfer ownership of the property.

Fuentes v. Shevin (1972)

The importance of notice and the right to be heard is an important check on the power of the government to deprive an individual of property, which is especially likely to be unfairly used when the government is acting on behalf of a private party. These due process protections must attach before the property is taken away, since the later return of the property does not compensate for its temporary wrongful deprivation.

Hurtado v. California (1884)

Due process of law in the 14th Amendment refers to that law of the land in each state which derives its authority from the inherent and reserved powers of the state, exerted within the limits of those fundamental principles of liberty and justice which lie at the base of all our civil and political institutions.

A State of Connecticut Supreme Court Decision

At the State of Connecticut Supreme Court level, in 2019, a tangential case concerning a home owner's property rights was won-in-part by the homeowner, and may serve as case law precedent for the home taxation situation.

In ENRICO MANGIAFICO v. TOWN OF FARMINGTON ET AL. (SC 19993), Mangiafico claims that by placing his house on the blight list (i.e., a home not maintained properly), and assessing fines and filing liens against him, the town illegally took his property in violation of the State and U.S. Constitutions. The court ruled as follows:

> *Pursuant to federal statute (42 U.S.C. § 1983), every person who, under color of any statute, ordinance or regulation of any state, subjects another person to the deprivation of constitutional rights, shall be liable to the injured party in an action at law or suit in equity.*

> *The plaintiff landowner, M, sought, inter alia, injunctive relief and to recover damages under 42 U.S.C. § 1983 from the named defendant, the Town of Farmington, among other defendants, alleging that the town's designation of M's property as blighted, its assessment of daily punitive fines, and its imposition of liens on his property constituted a taking in violation of the federal and state constitutions.*

The court ordered the case sent back to Superior Court, directing the court to grant Enrico his civil rights.

Summary

We the People

Everything *American* starts with "We the People"; people run the government, not the other way around. Authority over government is why "freedom of speech" exists. Unfettered dialogue amongst ourselves is essential in order for us to pilot our subordinate government apparatus.

"Freedom of speech", the right to influence the *political opinions* of others out in the public domain, has no restraints. This includes hate speech, agenda media, and even falsehoods claimed against public officials, so long as the optic is political (non-political falsehoods = defamation).

Today, the "originalists" who interpret the constitution as written, and the "evolutionists" who say it should be adopted to circumstances, both still agree that free speech sits above government authority. Inconsistently, the two camps part ways when it comes to property, even though property ownership stands elevated by the same "we the people" perch, an *inalienable right* – not able to be given or taken away by government.

Conservative Originalists maintain that Americans – not the government – fully own private property: American homes, our savings, our cars, etc., with inalienable *absolute* rights to property. Conversely, *Socialist Evolutionists* believe that property, unlike speech, stands sub-classified with *limited* rights, molded by the evolving needs of the government.

As things stand, the U.S. Constitution was never amended to sub-classify property, permitting open-ended taxation of homes (or cars) by municipalities. Such an amendment would repudiate the whole "We the People" foundation, placing us and our property below the government.

Instead, to circumvent this conundrum, and without a battle being waged over its legal standing, State Legislatures invented a tax lien/ confiscation extortion device, which simply ignores Constitutional protections of private property.

In the American system, which grew out of the English system, the highest set of rights are called *Natural Rights* - inalienable rights that cannot be taken or forfeited – possessed by every person regardless of stature or class. Natural Rights include one's uncompromised right to life, liberty and property, so long as no criminal behavior is in play. This principle was sanctified in the *Magna Carta*, back in 1215.

From this perch, a collection of unwritten *Common Laws* evolved, used for centuries to ensure that Natural Rights were upheld. Out of Common Law, the American founders crafted the *U.S. Constitution*, which more precisely articulates one's natural rights to life, liberty and property.

Below this, and subordinate to the U.S. Constitution, sit *Federal Statutes, State Constitutions* and *State Statutes,* many moving parts. Being subordinate, lower-level laws must not limit any rights found in the U.S. Constitution, though States can broaden rights locally. Nor can lower-level laws invent state powers (e.g. assessment-based taxes) which sit outside the bands of the U.S. Constitution

These lower-level legal bodies often violate the pecking order. State legislatures pass unconstitutional law, judges rule unconstitutionally, local mayors operate unconstitutionally (e.g. budget voting, tax sales), etc. Unless challenged at the U.S. Constitutional level, these illegal practices are allowed to stand, crushing the natural, sacred rights of the citizens.

The founders of both America and Connecticut set up a system to prevent all of this corruption. Somehow the worst violators of the U.S. Constitution became the states, who now seem a wall separating common citizens from their U.S. Constitutional protections.

State home taxation habits and local tax collectors must be confronted by the rule of law at the U.S. Constitution level. All of the legal points made in this paper sit at the federal level, hence ultimately it is the responsibility of the Department of Justice to adjudicate these matters. A plaintiff (The Town of Simsbury) and a defendant (The State of Connecticut) is all that is needed.